# 60 WAYS TO MAKE STRESS WORK FOR YOU

**Andrew E. Slaby, M.D., Ph.D., M.P.H.**

T·H·E
**PIA**
PRESS

™

BANTAM
NONFICTION

**BANTAM BOOKS**
NEW YORK · TORONTO · LONDON · SYDNEY · AUCKLAND

*This edition contains the complete text
of the original hardcover edition.*
NOT ONE WORD HAS BEEN OMITTED.

60 WAYS TO MAKE STRESS WORK FOR YOU

*A Bantam Nonfiction Book / published by arrangement with
The PIA Press*

PRINTING HISTORY
*PIA Press edition published 1988*
*Bantam edition / August 1991*

BANTAM NONFICTION *and the portrayal of a boxed "b" are trademarks
of Bantam Books, a division of Bantam Doubleday Dell Publishing
Group, Inc.*

ISBN 0-553-29209-9

*Published simultaneously in the United States and Canada*

---

*Bantam Books are published by Bantam Books, a division of Bantam
Doubleday Dell Publishing Group, Inc. Its trademark, consisting of the
words "Bantam Books" and the portrayal of a rooster, is Registered in
U.S. Patent and Trademark Office and in other countries. Marca
Registrada. Bantam Books, 666 Fifth Avenue, New York, New York
10103.*

---

PRINTED IN THE UNITED STATES OF AMERICA

OPM      0 9 8 7 6 5 4 3 2 1

# A CHINESE PROVERB ADVISES, "WELCOME CRISES"

The Chinese character for crisis is a combination of the characters for danger and opportunity. Crisis and stress allow us to see in bold relief that which creates who we are.

Bernard Baruch said that lost opportunity is life's greatest hell. We can learn from the pain and disappointment of a broken marriage, a complicated merchandising task, a life-threatening illness, or the end of an affair. We can discover why we act as we do, and use that knowledge to obtain more of what we want.

Fires that lead to burnout also fuel success. The effects of stress depend on how we handle it. This is the secret of successful people.

# CONTENTS

This book is not intended to replace personal medical care and/or professional supervision; there is no substitute for the experience and information that your doctor or mental health professional can provide. Rather, it is our hope that this book will provide additional information to help people understand the nature of stress and the physical and psychiatric conditions that can evolve.

Proper treatment should always be tailored to the individual. If you read something in this book that seems to conflict with your doctor or mental health professional's instructions, contact him/her. There may be sound reasons for recommending treatment that may differ from the information presented in this book.

If you have any questions about any treatment in this book, please consult your doctor or mental health care professional.

In addition, the names and cases used in this book do not represent actual people, but are composite cases drawn from several sources.

*"It is not the experience that happens to you;
it is what you do with the experience
that happens to you"*

*Bertrand Russell*

# Introduction

How many times have you heard, "Stress can kill," or, "Stress can cause burnout at work, in marriages, with children, and with ourselves."

Sure, it's a cliché, but it's too often true. Burnt-out people lack enthusiasm. Because of stress, they have lost both a sensitivity to the joy of life and the ability to cope with pain, boredom, or burden.

We all have stress throughout our lives. But not all stress is bad. The question is: how do we make stress work for us?

We can channel our stress to help us grow. Many well-known people have managed to do exactly that. Lee Iacocca turned the stress of being fired from his job at Ford into becoming the head of the Chrysler Corporation. Twenty years ago, First Lady Betty Ford handled her stress by drinking and abusing drugs. Today, she runs her own drug and alcohol abuse clinic. She was finally able to redirect her stress to work for her and others.

Stress can benefit our bodies and our minds. When we exercise, physical stress builds our muscles. Psychological stress builds friendships, marriages, and families. Artistic and entrepreneurial creativity are fueled by psychological stress. But to benefit from stress we must learn how to focus and manage it, to glean the positive and eliminate the negative.

There is an old Chinese proverb: "Welcome crises." The Chinese character for crisis is a combination of the characters for danger and opportunity. Crisis and stress allow us to see in bold relief the qualities that shape who we are... what our needs are, what our vulnerabilities are, and what we *could* be if we were able to make stress work for us rather than against us. Stress to a piece of fine crystal causes a crack which allows us to better determine its structure. Stress to the personality, according to Freud, allows us to better understand ourselves. When we are stressed, we can understand the biological, psychological, social, and existential parameters that converge to make us who we are. This allows an understanding of ourselves and an opportunity for growth that might not have been possible if the crisis had not occurred.

Bernard Baruch said that lost opportunity is life's greatest hell. We can learn from the pain and disappointment of a broken marriage, a complicated merchandising task, a life-threatening illness, or the end of an affair. We can discover why we act as we do, and use that knowledge to obtain more of what we want.

Fires that lead to burnout also fuel success. The effects of stress depend on how we handle it. When we use maximum exertion to master a challenging task, we increase the wear and tear on our coronary arteries, but we also enhance our self-esteem, self-efficiency, and the feeling that we are in control. This is the secret of successful people.

The trouble with success is that the formula for it is often the same for a nervous breakdown. That's why I've written this book. There is no reason that we all can't turn the formula around and make stress work for us!

# How to Use This Book

Controlling stress and making it work for us can be difficult. When stress is out of control, we can get hurt. Sometimes physical reactions to the stress in our lives can cause us permanent harm. This book will teach you ways to control your stress and how to use stress to your advantage. Read it all the way through. Pick out the ideas that appeal to you, expand upon them to meet your needs, and control the stress you encounter each day.

# 1

# A Stress Overview

Stress is inevitable. We are hired . . . and we are fired. We are promoted . . . and demoted. Marriages begin . . . and they end. In between there is the day-to-day struggle of living with someone, raising children, and making it all work. There is no way we can be alive and not experience it. When you're in a tense situation and you're experiencing stress, it's almost impossible to see beyond what you're feeling. You think that no one else could possibly be under as much stress as you are. But stress *is* universal.

# A National Health Problem

Forty percent of the U.S. population reportedly uses tranquilizers. One half to three quarters of routine medical practice is devoted to complaints relating to stress. Headaches, high blood pressure, accidents, alcoholism, ulcers, suicides, and heart attacks are just some of the many problems associated with stress.

Stress creates vicious cycles. Stressed people begin to skip lunch. They don't eat, and they don't share their problems with others. Poor diet reduces their ability to fight infections. Social isolation leads to depression. Stress accumulates and explodes in anger, leading to strains at work, and at home with wives, lovers, parents, and children. These emotional strains cause pain, and this pain can lead to alcohol and drug abuse—with disastrous consequences.

- At any given moment, at least ten percent of the American population has a significant alcohol or drug abuse problem.
- A staggering fifty percent of people in car accidents test positive for alcohol in their blood.

- Six out of ten car fatalities involving children under age 20 also involve alcohol use.

Even without alcohol, stress-related emotional upset occurring in the six hours prior to a car accident has been found to be a major factor in as many as twenty percent of traffic fatalities. How many more stressed people, preoccupied with problems, walk in front of oncoming cars or suffer falls or other accidents because of impaired concentration due to stress? Unfortunately, not even our children are immune to stress. In another study, the majority of accidental injuries of preschool children were found to occur during a time of family stress, such as a move to a new home.

## An Industrial Problem

Impaired judgment and concentration caused by substance abuse leads to accidents at work, at home, and on the road. Stress disorders cost industry upwards of $25 billion in absenteeism, reduced performance, and health benefit payments. And this figure pales when compared to the costs of stress-related alcohol and drug abuse in the workplace: a whopping $100 billion!

# 2

# *The Myths of Stress*

### *Myth #1:* Stress is ALWAYS bad.

This is perhaps the biggest myth that surrounds stress. Frequently stress can help us function. Whether we like it or not, some stress is essential in our lives—without it, we might not feel any motivation at all. Without the stress of having to pay bills, many people would elect to sleep rather than work. And without work, many of our greatest achievements would never be realized. Stress is not negative by definition; rather, it is our *control* of stress that determines whether or not it is harmful. If we are in control of our stress, then any stressful situation will be seen as a challenge—a challenge that can lead to positive results.

## *Myth #2:* **Stress prevents good performance.**

It is often thought that stress prevents good performance. But it can enhance performance as well. It has been said that skills to win the wars of Europe were learned on the playing fields of Eton. Sports and the military are said to build men...and women. Jogging builds leg muscles and increases the heart's ability to handle both physical and mental stress. While many seek to reduce stress in order to perform better at work or at home, we also know that a modicum of anxiety is needed to study for an examination or drive a car defensively. Mild to moderate stress enhances functioning, for example, in sports, music, even sex.

### *Myth #3:* **Only tragedies cause stress.**

Some people believe that stress only comes from major disasters in our lives, such as death, illness, taxes, divorce, or job loss. Conversely, what many would consider to be a positive event can, in reality, be a source of stress.

Marriage, moving, or having a child can produce stress that, to some people, is equal to or greater than many tragic losses they have experienced. The birth of a child is a joyous occasion, but any of us who are parents know that there may be mixed blessings— ranging from loss of sleep during the first few months of parenthood to ever-mounting college tuition bills.

Job promotion, certainly a positive event, can also bring some negative results. Along with the increase in status and money can come increased responsibility, deadlines, and loneliness. Job advancement means more accountability, and the chance that more people will be angry at you when things don't go the right way.

### *Myth #4:* **Stress is a loser's problem.**

Another myth about stress is that the person "at the top" is immune to it. Most of the time, people "at the top" are held more accountable for their failures than their successes. When things go well, everyone shares in the success. But when there's a disaster—a bankruptcy, for example—we look for a culprit. He or she is usually the person "at the top." In a business, the buck stops with the boss. If a firm is large, the boss may be accountable to a board of directors and countless shareholders. If a company gets sued, the person in charge may be named in the suit. If a corporation begins to fail, the top executive may be fired.

## *Myth #5:* **Only winners have stress.**

Many people believe the exact opposite of Myth #4; namely, they see stress as a problem *only* for the person at the top. They picture a top executive working twenty-four hours a day, ulcers eating away at his insides, constantly being bombarded with life-and-death decisions, meeting with twenty shareholders, *and* yelling into five telephones— all at the same time! However, studies of top executives suggest that those in high-pressure jobs are often better at coping with stress than teachers, nurses, policemen, firemen, telephone operators, and factory workers. Some theorize that this is due to the fact that those with the most skill in adapting to stress rise to the top—sort of a corporate survival of the fittest.

Another explanation is that people who are at the top of an organization have more power to control their environment. It's easier to handle pressure if we feel we have the power to make some changes—we accept more readily what we cannot control by controlling what we can. For example, an executive can ask his or her secretary to "hold my calls" and then take a breather from the pressure by meditating or taking a short nap. But the secretary doesn't have the same luxury of being able to control the work environment.

We often think that people at the top have more heart attacks because of stress. While the risk of having a heart attack appears to rise along with occupational status, results of studies have been inconclusive. Some researchers have found that the risk of heart attack declines as salary levels increase— or that there is no relationship at all between what you earn and your chances of having a heart attack.

# 3

## *The Stress Test*

How can you tell if stress is creating problems for you? Are there warning signs that you should be aware of? Here is a simple Stress Test that will let you know how big a part stress plays in your life. This Stress Test will help you measure your stress index (the signs of stress in your life). By the way, taking this test shouldn't be the cause of stress, because there are no right or wrong answers! No one will be giving you a grade, so just be honest.

## The Stress Test

Which of the following do you answer yes to? Each "Yes" answer counts as one point. Each "No" answer counts as zero points.

**DO YOU:** *Yes* *No*

1. Ignore introspection or self-examination, preferring not to know what really makes you tick? ___ ___

2. Drink lots of caffeine? ___ ___

3. Neglect vitamins, when you know they might improve your physical and emotional sense of well being? ___ ___

4. Disregard salt intake? ___ ___

5. Skip meals? ___ ___

6. Do everything yourself, rather than asking for and accepting help from others? ___ ___

7. Ignore other people's suggestions, for fear of admitting that you might not always have the right answers? ___ ___

8. Blow up over trivial annoyances instead of putting them in perspective and moving on? ___ ___

|  | *Yes* | *No* |
|---|---|---|

9. Seek unrealistic goals, dooming yourself to failure? ___ ___

10. Lack a plan? ___ ___

11. Not take time to relax muscles? ___ ___

12. Have to be reminded that laughter is one of the best ways we have to get through the day? ___ ___

13. Act rude when other behavior is appropriate? ___ ___

14. Not know your values? ___ ___

15. Ignore your body's signals, denying that you could be tired, overworked, or even sick? ___ ___

16. Deny reality? ___ ___

17. Fail to test stress tolerance? ___ ___

18. Make a "big deal" out of a lot of little things, obsessing rather than viewing them as a small part of a bigger, better picture? ___ ___

19. Discount meditation? ___ ___

|     |     | *Yes* | *No* |
|-----|-----|-------|------|

20. Follow the path of others, \_\_\_\_ \_\_\_\_
    when you're having trouble
    finding your own way?

21. Have difficulty making de- \_\_\_\_ \_\_\_\_
    cisions?

22. Lack knowledge of your \_\_\_\_ \_\_\_\_
    strengths and weaknesses?

23. Lack organization in your \_\_\_\_ \_\_\_\_
    personal or professional life?

24. Minimize encounters with \_\_\_\_ \_\_\_\_
    people and ideas different
    from yours?

25. Avoid crises, seeing only the \_\_\_\_ \_\_\_\_
    negative and not the posi-
    tive effects that can evolve
    as a result?

26. Keep everything inside, \_\_\_\_ \_\_\_\_
    rather than sharing your
    thoughts and fears with
    loved ones or friends?

27. Lack imagination? \_\_\_\_ \_\_\_\_

28. Not belong to a support \_\_\_\_ \_\_\_\_
    group, even though you
    could benefit from sharing
    your experiences and con-

cerns with others who have
been there?

29. Not exercise, even though      ___   ___
you know it can make you
feel and look better?

30. Lack interpersonal skills?      ___   ___

31. Not seek help for stress-       ___   ___
related symptoms such as
headache, stomachache, in-
ability to sleep, grinding
teeth, or facial twitches?

32. Think yoga, Zen, and self-      ___   ___
hypnosis are silly, and could
not be meaningful in your
life?

33. Feel your life is out of con-   ___   ___
trol?

34. Fail to leave time for the      ___   ___
unexpected?

35. Minimize rest?                  ___   ___

36. Not remember when you           ___   ___
were last massaged?

37. Not create buffer zones be-     ___   ___
fore and after anticipated
stresses?

|     |                                                                                  | *Yes* | *No* |
|-----|----------------------------------------------------------------------------------|-------|------|
| 38. | Find yourself waiting for someone and getting angry, even though you know that person's often late? | ___   | ___  |
| 39. | Think everyone is replaceable?                                                   | ___   | ___  |
| 40. | Procrastinate?                                                                   | ___   | ___  |
| 41. | Hide your weaknesses?                                                            | ___   | ___  |
| 42. | Find yourself spending a lot of time lamenting the past?                        | ___   | ___  |
| 43. | Not believe in the spiritual?                                                   | ___   | ___  |
| 44. | Find yourself unprepared?                                                       | ___   | ___  |
| 45. | Dress down?                                                                      | ___   | ___  |
| 46. | Think spending time on yourself is a waste of time?                             | ___   | ___  |
| 47. | Have only one right way— your way—to do something?                              | ___   | ___  |
| 48. | Never really let yourself go, always mindful of what others will think of you?  | ___   | ___  |
| 49. | Say yes to everything, rather than risk the conflict of disagreement?           | ___   | ___  |
| 50. | Gossip?                                                                          | ___   | ___  |

|  | *Yes* | *No* |
|---|---|---|

51. Race through the day, never taking the time to "smell the roses?" ___ ___

52. Turn the TV on as soon as you enter the house? ___ ___

53. Abhor routine? ___ ___

54. Fail to communicate roles in routine, resulting in continual dissatisfaction with how family members and coworkers function? ___ ___

55. Frequently encounter surprises, for which you feel unprepared? ___ ___

56. Ignore where you live and how your office and house are arranged? ___ ___

57. Refuse to accept that advances in technology, such as beepers, mobile phones, and answering machines, can ease the stress of time away from your home or office? ___ ___

58. Let friends "happen" to you, rather than going through a selection process? ___ ___

|  | Yes | No |
|---|---|---|

59. Feel you have to please everyone, never really pleasing yourself? ___ ___

60. Frequently feel like you are caught in a whirlpool, unable to get out? ___ ___

61. Feel powerless to make a change in your life? ___ ___

62. Feel afraid to take chances, to surprise people? ___ ___

The closer your "Yes" total is to sixty-two, the higher your stress index and the greater your need to employ some of the techniques discussed in this book.

# 4

# *What Causes Stress?*

*Stressors* are the source of all stress. They are defined as anything that causes your body to react physiologically or psychologically. A stressor could be a bright light, a loud noise, an exciting basketball game, or your boss screaming at you. By itself, a stressor is neither positive nor negative. How you react to these stressors determines whether your stress becomes negative or positive.

*Negative* stress arises from social, psychological, or physical situations that we feel are beyond our control. This type of stress produces either unintended or undesired results. Quite simply, we lose our ability to cope. Then these stressful situations build into subtle pressures that envelop and, at times, overwhelm us—testing the fiber of which we are made. Continued negative stress can also diminish our resistance to other stressors, causing a "snowball effect." That's why it's important to pay attention to stress.

*Positive* stress can result from many of the same situations that cause negative stress. The difference is how you view that stress and the subsequent way your body reacts to the stressors. Paying attention to a potential source of stress, and properly dealing with it, is one way to turn it to your advantage. When you are in control, your body doesn't overreact, and the same stressful situation will be seen as a challenge, not a threat. For example, your boss screaming doesn't have to upset you. It can challenge and motivate you to achieve greater success and happiness at work and at home.

You have a 1:00 doctor's appointment. You know you'll have to wait—you've had to wait at least thirty minutes every time you've seen this physician. How do you deal with the stress? You can wait angrily in the waiting room, pacing, calling your office several times, complaining to the receptionist about punctuality, how busy you are, how you'll leave in five minutes if you're not taken. Or you can use the half hour to listen to music on a headset you brought, catch up on some reading, or try some meditation.

Call ahead and see how late the doctor is running, or take the first appointment of the day. The point is that you can mitigate the stress by rearranging the stressors to suit your lifestyle.

# 5

# *What Happens During Stress*

In prehistoric times, when Neanderthal man was threatened, his brain began a series of reactions designed to protect him. His heart beat faster, his blood pressure rose, his muscles received more oxygen, his blood sugar level increased, his pupils dilated, his digestion decreased, and his perspiration flowed. These physiological changes increased his alertness, preparing him to act on one of his two options: stay and fight, or run for his life.

The physical reactions that prehistoric man experienced when he felt anxiety and fear are referred to as the *"fight-or-flight"* syndrome.

Although our environment has changed, we still have the physiology and fears of our primitive ancestors. We have the same age-old physical responses to stress. Even when we're not in mortal danger, our bodies react as if we were. We feel our heart racing. Our blood pressure rises. In the extreme, we suffer "splitting headaches," chest pain, or heart attacks.

But, unless we find ourselves in physical danger, these fight-or-flight responses aren't very helpful. Assault or retreat are not usually recommended as the best ways to cope with the pressures of deadlines, bosses, clients, colleagues, patients, spouses, parents, and children. Without a proper avenue of release, the physical changes caused by our fight-or-flight response may have detrimental effects. For example, the high blood pressure that occurs in the *fight-or-flight* syndrome, if repeated frequently without relief over long periods of time, can result in a state of consistently high blood pressure. This, in turn, can lead to a wide range of harmful conditions, from heart disease to stroke to kidney failure.

Stress as a "diagnosis" can be many things to many different doctors. A cardiologist, a gynecologist, an internist, a pediatrician, and a psychiatrist may all diagnose and treat stress differently. For example, the heart patient may be warned away from all stressful activities and given medication. Women suffering from panic attacks and anxiety are often "misdiagnosed" as under stress from pressures at home and work. They may be given mild tranquilizers without real regard to whether their stress reactions are psychological or physiological. Internists and even psychiatrists are also guilty of the same "it's in your head" diagnosis. Those who think they are suffering from stress should insist that their doctor do a complete biological work-up to determine whether their stress is caused by any underlying physiological cause.

# 6

# *What Stress Can Do*

Age, sex, background, heredity, social make-up, and the accumulated wear and tear on our bodies all determine how we experience stress. Symptoms of stress are provided in Table 1 and the illnesses associated with stress in Table 2. These range from heart attacks and ulcers to depression, trauma, suicide, anxiety disorders, and alcohol and drug abuse. Even cancer can be caused by stress. Stress can lead to smoking and heavy drinking. The former is a risk factor for lung cancer; the latter for cancers of the mouth, throat, esophagus, and stomach. In addition, stress impairs our immune response, leading not only to decreased ability to fight infection, but also to reject cancer cells.

## Table 1
## Stress Symptoms

Absenteeism
Alcohol use (excessive) or dependence
Anger (chronic)
Argumentative behavior
Backaches
Boredom
Bruxism (grinding teeth)
Car accidents (or near-misses)
Compulsions
Depersonalization
Diarrhea
Dietary problems
Dread of getting out of bed
Drug use and dependence
Dysattention (impaired attention)
Dyspepsia (indigestion)
Fatigue
Headache
Hyperexcitation
Hypersomnia (oversleeping)
Imperiousness
Impulsiveness
Inefficiency
Infections (frequent)
Insomnia
Irritability
Low self-esteem

Malaise
Muscle aches
Muscle weakness
Obsessions
Pain without physical causes
Palpitations
Poor judgment
Rigidity
Sexual dysfunction
Sinking stomach (nausea)
Smoking
Social withdrawal
Suicide attempts
Tachypnea (rapid, shallow breathing)
Tardiness
Tearfulness
Trauma
Urination (frequent)
Vomiting (frequent)

## Table 2
### Stress Illnesses

Alcoholism
Anorexia nervosa
Aphthous ulcers (canker sores)
Arthritis
Asthma
Bulimia nervosa
Cancer
Cardiac arrhythmias
Colitis
Coronary heart disease
Depression
Dermatitis (inflammation of the skin)
Drug abuse and dependence
Duodenal and gastric ulcers
Hypercholesterolemia (high cholesterol)
Hypertension
Mania
Migraine headaches
Panic disorders
Phobias
Premenstrual tension
Sciatica
Tension headaches

# 7

## *60 Ways to Make Stress Work For You*

We live in a stress-filled world. Crowded cities, noise and air pollution, isolation, loneliness, and the constant "bad" news reported in the media, press in on all of us. The fear of AIDS and herpes, the threat of a nuclear holocaust, interest rates and inflation, worries about aging and financial security, failing friendships and, at times, just boredom add up. All are stresses that, taken together, may one day break the proverbial camel's back. We all find ourselves at times shouting, "Stop the world, I want to get off!" but most of us don't.

Why not? Because most of us don't really want to "get off," rather, we want to live happy, relatively stress-free lives. You *can* choose a better way than simply shouting at the heavens (or family or friends) in vain. This chapter lays out sixty simple strategies you can use to make stress work for you. These strategies are designed to help you with concrete suggestions, and inspire you to design at least sixty more ways of your own.

Turn back to the Stress Test you took on pages 24–30. When going through the next section, pay special attention to the questions you answered yes to, since many of the sixty questions correspond to some of the sixty ways that follow.

# I. General Ideas

Here are some general thoughts to get you started turning the stress in your life to your advantage. These are techniques that you can use every day that will eventually become habits, and you'll wonder why you never used them before.

# 1. Organize.

Disorganization begets chaos and stress. Organization introduces an element of predictability. Predictability leads to control. When things are out of control, we are stressed. Stress is reduced when we can control what is happening. Organize your personal life, set up a schedule that you can reasonably expect to meet, make a list of what you have to do, and follow it! Don't overextend, just organize before you act. And remember . . . the best laid plans can change, so be flexible. Give yourself plenty of time for each activity. If you're running late or things get cancelled, relax! You're prepared.

## 2. Seek Opportunity from Crises.

Studies indicate that those who cope with stress without dire physiological consequences see crises as opportunities. If the worst happened and we survived, or better yet, learned how to cope despite the worst, the rest is easy. If something bad happens, think how to use it to make things better. We reduce our stress when we use it as a teacher. It's the proverbial glass that's half empty or half full. You can emerge from a devastating event stronger, more confident, and more in touch with who you are and what you really want and need.

## 3. Create Environments that Reduce Stress.

There is no doubt that color can have a powerful impact on our emotional state. We use color to describe moods, feelings, thoughts: feeling in the pink or a little blue; seeing red; having black days; etc. A German psychologist reported that children performed better on certain types of tests in rooms that were painted light blue, yellow, yellow-green, or orange. Those in rooms painted white, black, or brown seemed duller and less responsive.

Should we all paint our homes orange and yellow? Obviously not. But our surroundings influence how we feel and how we function. It is ironic that so little thought has gone into the color of the walls, floor coverings, furniture, and artwork that fill our worksites. Colors can reduce stress and create a sense of well-being. When an environment engenders dignity, a number of difficult tasks become more achievable. Reducing environmental stress allows us to be objective, to focus our efforts, and to be efficient and productive. Alien environments alienate the worker not only from the workplace, but also from the work task. Caring is expressed by the presence of a pleasant environment, whether at home or at work.

## 4. Take Control of Your Life.

A man seeking help for the emotional turmoil created by a divorce stated he had not been to the theater in ten years because his wife would not go. He blamed his wife for all the plays he had missed. It never occurred to him that he had control over this decision—that he could have gone to the theater alone or with his friends.

While interest in the theater is seldom a critical element of a successful marriage, interest in open and honest discussion is a necessity. Even when we have good communication in a marriage, we can't expect our spouse to give us everything we need. If, for example, someone hates the theater, odds are it may take her a long time to change her mind. Unless they're faced with a crisis, people are usually slow to change. It's up to us to assume responsibility for getting what we want.

It's easier to blame someone else for our unhappiness and failure. But making excuses doesn't solve anything. Being a "victim" is a convenient excuse for not taking responsibility for our actions and moving ahead. For us to grow, the first step is to identify our goals. The second step is to determine what actions we can realistically take to achieve them.

People who do not suffer from stress see a crisis as a challenge and an opportunity. Those who best manage stress feel in control of their lives.

## 5. Leave Time for the Unexpected.

The very unexpectedness of many life events—like death, illness, or financial ruin or success—makes them noxious for us. People have a remarkable ability to cope. But coping requires time. We need time to accurately perceive a crisis and time to rally our internal and external resources. Initially denying and minimizing the full impact of many stressful life events often allows the opportunity to use more time to gather the resources we need to cope.

# 6. Don't Procrastinate.

Delaying anything means added stress. By postponing studying for an exam, you make stress worse through the increased anxiety of not having the time to master difficult material. By procrastinating, you simply won't have the time to marshal all of your resources. Furthermore, you won't have the time to handle any of life's unexpected—and unwelcomed—surprises. You never win by increasing stress with delay. Instead, you are seen as a failure, as someone who does not work effectively.

Most people don't put off things they enjoy doing. We procrastinate because the task is "not fun" (writing a report) or possibly painful (going to the dentist) or because we are too busy. The most successful people approach every task or activity as it appears. Experience has shown them that putting something off until the last minute can only make it more complicated and stressful. Most "reformed" procrastinators have learned that once the unwanted task is completed, they have more time to enjoy the things they really want to do.

## 7. Forget the Past.

This may seem contrary to popular concepts of psychoanalysis, but there is some truth to the cliche: "Today is the first day of the rest of your life." We cannot change the past. Freud felt that neurosis entailed trying to change in the present that which could only be changed in the past. What your mother and father didn't give you can't be obtained from your spouse or lover. Don't choose your life partner with the hope that you're finally getting the parent you never had—it won't work. It's a good bet that if you really have found someone just like your parents, then you have also found someone who probably can't give you what you want. To get what you need, you will have to seek partners (and alternatives) in the present. We can learn from the past. We can take comfort from the past. But we cannot re-live it.

## 8. Minimize Surprise.

You'll experience enough surprises in life without creating new ones. In today's world of instant information, make use of TV, news radio, 800 numbers, to get the latest updates that can help minimize stressful delays. For example, it should come as no surprise that airports can be a hassle. If you must walk a long distance in an airport you may need to check your luggage through. On the other hand, checking luggage through may mean it gets lost, and lost luggage is gained stress. As an alternative to lugging heavy parcels long distances (and possibly straining muscles and slipping disks), invest in a baggage carrier. If you plan the right way you can minimize surprise—and stress.

## 9. Choose Friends Carefully.

George Eliot said that the strongest principle of growth lies in human choice. This is the strongest principle of stress reduction. Choosing the right companions is the key. It enables us to share our quandaries, increase our strengths, and create innovative solutions for life's inevitable adversities. We need people around us who support us when we take stress-filled risks. Why not choose the best with whom we work, with whom we play, and with whom we make love? Why not? We can all tolerate much more stress in life when the right people are there to let us know that we are not alone.

## II. Get to Know Yourself— The Physical Side

Beating stress frequently involves controlling forces that can harm you physically. Often we don't even recognize the damage that stress can do to our bodies until it's much too late. Here are some ways to keep stress from ruining your overall health.

## 10. Examine Yourself.

Before you can reduce stress or make it work for you, you must recognize its signs and identify its sources. Monitor yourself physically and psychologically (pp. 40–42). Take an inventory of your life style:

- Are you always tired?
- Is your alcohol intake increasing?
- Are you more irritable at work or at home?
- Is your interest in sex, art, good conversation, and food decreasing?
- Do you dread going to work?
- Is there no longer any joy in life?
- Do you ever feel that if you didn't wake up in the morning, maybe you'd be better off?

If you can confront these very difficult questions, you will be able to begin the process of making stress work for you. If you answer "yes" to any of these questions, its time to begin your examination. Look at your answers honestly and seek solutions as soon as possible.

## 11. Recognize Early Signs
   of Stress Illness
   and Get Treated.

To avoid the consequences of stress we must monitor ourselves, take good care of ourselves, *and* let others care for us. What we may think of as "understandable depression" after the stress of losing a business deal may not be depression. There are many potentially serious conditions that mimic depression, such as hypothyroidism and cancer, that may only be diagnosed with a thorough physical. But if we don't recognize the signs of stress, and if we don't rely on others to help us, the underlying cause of our problem may go undetected.

In general, if recognized early, physiological ravages of stress that are not caused by another medical condition can be prevented or reversed (see pp. 40–42). Are we drinking more than we usually do? Smoking more? Sleeping less? Crying more? Recognizing the early warning signs of stress allows us to prevent the more serious anxiety, panic, or even depression that may follow. Other problems that may result from unrecognized stress are: weight gain, decreased sleep, and increased use of drugs and alcohol.

## 12. Reduce Xanthine Intake.

While good meals with good friends reduce stress, there are a number of things we eat that increase stress by countering the forces of relaxation. These substances include xanthines (such as coffee, tea, and cola drinks) and other stimulants, which mimic the stress-related changes induced by cocaine and amphetamines, such as increased heart rate, blood pressure, and oxygen demand on the heart. For example, excess coffee drinking leads to caffeinism, a state characterized by anxiety leading to panic, insomnia, palpitations, tachycardia (rapid heart rate), diarrhea, and irregular heartbeat.

# 13. Avoid Vitamin Depletion.

We need optimal levels of vitamins for our nervous and endocrine (glandular) systems to function, especially at stressful times. Particularly important are: vitamin C (citrus fruit, juices, tomatoes); thiamine (vitamin B1) (whole grain cereals, peas, beans, peanuts); riboflavin (vitamin B2) (eggs, green vegetables, lean meat, liver, and kidney); niacin (fish, legumes, whole grain cereals, yeast); pantothenic acid (vitamin B5); pyridoxine (vitamin B6) (blackstrap molasses, meat, cereal grains, wheat germ); and choline.

Absence of these vitamins is associated with cardiovascular, neurological, and psychiatric problems, reducing our ability to cope with stress. Vitamin depletion symptoms include depression, anxiety, muscle weakness, gastric upset, and insomnia.

## 14. Monitor Salt Intake.

Salt depletion leads to weakness; salt excess to fluid retention. Excess fluid retention leads to central nervous system irritability, as well as high blood pressure. A low-salt diet is part of the management of hypertension to avoid heart attack and stroke. Elimination of excess salt use, or use of a salt substitute, reduces risk of these problems.

## 15. Avoid Hypoglycemia.

Hypoglycemia, or low blood sugar, is manifested by increased cardiac activity, anxiety, irritability, light-headedness, and tremors. Some people with histories of diabetes in the family are particularly prone to reactive hypoglycemia. In this condition, blood sugar falls to dangerously low levels three to five hours after eating. In extreme cases, seizures occur. In less severe instances, a person feels irritable and angry. Eating small, regular amounts of food prevents this. Reactive hypoglycemia is brought on by ingestion of a large amount of carbohydrate in a limited amount of time.

People "on the go" or "on the fast track" often miss meals, reducing their ability to tolerate stress and to respond in a critical manner without impaired judgment and concentration. The testiness seen with those who miss meals can lead to friction with fellow employees, clients, friends, and family. Eating regular and well-balanced meals and avoiding excess sugar and processed food reduces the chances of hypoglycemia occurring.

## 16. Employ Biofeedback.

Control over a body function entails enhanced awareness of any change in that function. One technique, progressive muscle relaxation, will be discussed in Section VI. Awareness of how muscles feel when we alternately contract and relax them allows us to feel the impact of relaxation.

Comparably, through biofeedback (a high-tech approach in which an individual is hooked up to a series of monitors that allows him/her to see the actual progression of his/her bodily functions) we may learn to employ the awareness of our heart rate and blood pressure to lower both of these functions. Even skin temperature can be controlled by this technique. By getting "in touch" with our bodies, we learn who and what makes us feel good and bad. In this way, we can seek out those who help rather than hinder us in achieving our goals.

## 17. Exercise.

Exercise strengthens our cardiovascular system, our lungs, and our muscles. There is no question about the benefit of exercise to overall productivity and well being. In fact many companies now have either fitness centers, inter-company athletic programs, or aerobic exercise classes to increase employee fitness, thus reducing stress-related illness. It's been proven that even moderate walking can have cardiovascular benefits. While exercise cannot usually reverse already existing damage, it can keep us in the best possible condition to resist stress. Walking and jogging are not only good exercise but also provide time alone to review a situation and explore creative options.

## 18. Use Psychoactive Medications Appropriately.

Antianxiety agents and sleep medications can quickly reduce stress, but can also lead to more stress through drug dependence, decreased functioning, and problems with concentration and lethargy. Antidepressants, mood stabilizers, and tranquilizers—when properly prescribed after a careful evaluation—reduce stress by allowing us to function at our best. Using medications properly does not, by the way, mean you will have to use them forever. Most people become stable and can function drug free after a period of treatment, if the medication is properly prescribed to begin with.

Conversely, untreated psychiatric illness stresses both the person who struggles with it and those around him.

# 19. Get Rest.

This seems obvious, but is perhaps the most violated principle of all. Everyone knows that athletes must rest prior to the Olympics. So why shouldn't executive athletes rest prior to corporate olympics? Whether our confrontation is an athletic event or a corporate maneuver, the same physiological changes are activated in our bodies. No matter if we are teachers, parents, or salesmen, we all require rest so that our energy is at maximum levels when we need it.

After a confrontation, no matter what the cause, we need rest to recoup our resources. Getting enough rest can be extremely beneficial for our bodies. For example, bed rest, by allowing our hearts to require less oxygen and our muscles to relax, is one of the best antidotes to rising blood pressure.

# III. Self-Awareness and Emotions

It's vital to develop *self-awareness* as you take steps to reduce stress. Look inward and be aware of the things that you are doing to yourself that can increase your stress.

## 20. Choose Options that Are Realistic.

Some things are to be understood and changed. Others can only be understood. This is a paraphrasing of the *Serenity Prayer* of Alcoholics Anonymous: "Lord, grant me the courage to change what I can, the serenity to accept what I cannot, and the wisdom to know the difference."

We can accept what we cannot change by changing what we can. Options are not infinite. They vary for people by age, gender, and circumstance. Our challenge is to expand our options, regardless of our circumstances.

Stress may make us choose an option that will ease our pain in the short run, but ultimately cause dissatisfaction. Making choices that are reasonable, such as buying a house within our means, or setting price estimates based on realistic labor and material cost, help us to reduce stress.

## 21. Maximize Information Input.

It is easiest to formulate a realistic plan of action when you have the most information. When approaching a stressful situation, take the time to research all of your options. Try to understand the reasons that caused the stressful situation to occur in the first place. Fear of stress, and therefore stress itself, is reduced by knowing what stresses to antici- pate and how to manage them. For example, if you want to change careers, or re-enter the workplace, but are afraid to take a change, think carefully about what it is you really want and what you're currently unhappy with. Speak to people who have made a change. Get their advice. Do some research. By getting all the information that you can, not only will you have a more realistic view of what the possibilities are, but you'll know how to be prepared for them.

## 22. Develop a Plan and Goal.

You have to have a dream to make a dream come true. Stress exists when we don't know where we are going, or, if we do, we don't know how to get there. A plan reduces helplessness and allows us mini-goals to reach on the way to a long-term one. Alternative plans—a diversified portfolio, so to speak—reduces stress by not predicating self-esteem, success, or happiness upon achievement of a single goal. Make lists of priorities, goals, and realistic strategies for achieving them.

## 23. Know Your Values.

Knowing what is important to our existence and what is not allows us to focus our efforts on finding ways of coping. Experiences as diverse as surviving a concentration camp or a struggle with cancer have shown that when people find a reason to live, they will find a way to live.

## 24. Be Aware of Your Strengths and Weaknesses.

Knowing what you do well and what you don't can reduce stress. Simply admitting you have limitations frees you from potential negative stress because you don't have to do everything by yourself. You know when to ask for help and how to work with other people as a team. If you had to win a rugby match by yourself, you would lose the game. In any venture, stress is reduced when people work together toward a common goal.

## 25. Don't Say Yes to Everything.

Focusing on what you do best, and taking the time to do it right, will help you alleviate stress. Saying "yes" all the time won't work for long. It may avert an initial confrontation, but over time you could become angry, resentful, over-extended, even more stressed. It may seem easier, but in the end you will lose what you have accomplished. In the long run, you will realize that what you have lost is control of your life—and that can cause a lot of stress! If your answer is always "yes," then your choices are not free—instead, they are forced upon you by circumstance.

Your *emotions* play a large part in stress reduction, and when they are out of control, stress can run amok. Here are some ideas to help you keep your emotions in check.

## 26. Release Anger Appropriately.

Anger, like sexual desire, is normal. Both need release. Frustration leads to anger. Anger enhances and begets stress. Talking about anger with a friend, changing that which has made you angry, or dissipating anger in physical activity (such as playing squash) helps to reduce the dangerous consequences of anger. Driving a car fast or screaming at your spouse, children, or employees is destructive. Jogging until you feel better or simply screaming in a room alone after everyone has gone home are better alternatives. Write an angry letter, read it, and then throw it out!

## 27. Face Reality.

Be objective. There are things we cannot change. Growing old and dying are two facts of life that we can't alter. Denying inevitable facts can cause us to lose valuable time, time we need to reach our goals effectively.

Spending valuable time trying to make an unpleasant fact into something more palatable to us creates stress. Facing the facts objectively and working with them reduces stress by minimizing wasted energy (i.e., "spinning our wheels"). Standing back from a mountain allows us to better see a pass.

## 28. Reduce the Burden of Stress by Stress Inoculation.

A major stress may be reduced by breaking it down into masterable tasks over time. A trip is made up of many miles; not all are accomplished in a second.

For example, many people find Christmas to be a particularly stressful time of year. They become weighed down by the burden of expectations: buying and wrapping presents, buying and sending cards, decorating, parties, and meals. A simple way to reduce this annual agony is to buy Christmas gifts and wrap them in July and write Christmas cards in October. These suggestions may seen absurd, but they certainly leave more time for decorating and parties in December!

## 29. Normalize a Situation.

Stress is often created when we must hide part or all of something. A newly married woman was suspected of infidelity by her husband because of her excessive and unaccounted for time away from home. She felt her husband would reject her if he knew the truth: both her parents were alcoholic and she had to take care of them. She finally revealed her secret, and her husband was happy to learn she was not having an affair, and quite willing to help her. The young wife felt relieved of a stressful burden.

When a potentially alienating situation is brought out into the open, pressure is reduced. When someone knows you are a recovering alcoholic, they better understand the need for time to attend AA meetings and they won't force drinks on you. Knowing someone is gay reduces pressure to date or marry, or to perform better heterosexually.

## 30. Practice Imaging.

When stress appears or is anticipated, visualize in your mind how you will handle it, how you have handled it in the past, or how someone else you respect has successfully coped with it. This is the principle of support groups and the role of mentors in career development. We learn how to respond to stress from those who already have. This saves us many knocks from the cruel school of experience.

# 31. Join a Support Group.

If one doesn't exist, form one. Support groups for friends and relatives of a suicide discuss how they have learned to cope with the loss. Post-mastectomy support groups provide models of how to handle the stress of living with cancer or a husband's or lover's response to a mastectomy. Support groups for professionals play a role in suggesting alternatives for coping with the stresses of being a physician, lawyer, corporate director, teacher, or other professional. When we are stressed, we are often blinded to ways to reduce that stress—we get stuck in a rut and can't see a way out. Other people's solutions provide options for us. In addition, the strength of others in a support group buffers us when we face a stressful situation.

## 32. Carry Stress Reducers.

Stress is created whenever we feel out of control or when control is taken from us. If you anticipate that a plane will be delayed or that a friend will be late, try bringing some work with you so you don't waste time. If you get something accomplished, not only will you feel better, but you will also be less angry at your friend for the delay. If you find visiting someone stressful, bring a friend along to neutralize the situation. Even if bringing a friend doesn't reduce the stress, at least you'll have someone to ventilate with after a particularly nasty encounter.

## 33. Reduce Noise and People Pollution.

This is especially true for people who live in a city, but it applies to everyone. Do you feel surrounded by unwelcomed people and unpleasant sounds? If your productivity is decreasing because city noise is driving you berserk, move to the country. Get soundproof windows or move to a quieter street. Sleep with earplugs or headphones. Keep your windows closed and use air-conditioning, if possible. Unplug your phone for a few hours. Whenever possible, schedule your driving for the hours when traffic is lightest. We all need a safe haven, and it's up to us to create it.

## 34. Establish Routine.

Routine decreases stress by reducing the time spent on deciding what to do and how to do it. You need to establish priorities and routines to get things done efficiently. You'll waste less time and energy. For example, establishing routines can help you get a good night's sleep, and a quicker start in the morning. You can make it a pattern to start to unwind one hour before bedtime, so that you're relaxed when you want to go to sleep. Deciding what you're going to wear the night before can save you time and anxiety in the morning.

# IV. Social/Interpersonal Relationships

When we are under stress from any source often our relationships with friends, lovers, and families can break down just when we need their support the most. Take a moment to consider some ways to keep the people we value the most from being victims or sources of our stress.

## 35. Maintain a Sense of Humor.

Often we cause our own stress when we lose perspective, due to family, economic or other pressures. As Oscar Wilde said, "Life is far too important to take seriously." Put another way, the reason angels fly is that they take themselves lightly! We are all human beings, struggling. One hundred years from now, few of us will be remembered. While the struggling people we once were will be forgotten, hopefully our achievements will live on. This message is simple: As important as every day seems to be, in the immortal words of Scarlett O'Hara in *Gone with the Wind: "Tomorrow is another day!"* Remember to live life in the present tense, and your external stress will be kept in proper perspective.

## 36. Politeness Reduces Stress.

When we are polite to others, they will be polite to us. In other words, the old adage, "Do unto others . . ." can also help us reduce stress. Sometimes a thank-you, a door opened, or a smile is really welcome. Remember, how others treat us also affects our self-image. Why not keep our self-image positive by being courteous to others? When we take the time to work positively or constructively with our peers, it acts as a reinforcer to our own sense of self.

## 37. Be Assertive.

Take control. The great Rabbi Hillel taught us, "If I am not for myself, who is for me? If I am only for myself, who am I? If not now, when?" Stress increases when we look to others to make things happen, or simply sit back and wait. This makes us victims of circumstance. Be proactive rather than reactive.

Taking control of your life, your job, or any other source of stress reduces stress, neutralizing the negative energy that accompanies stress. Furthermore, your self-esteem is enhanced through controlling the way things happen.

## 38. Make Decisions.

Persevering in a hopeless cause increases stress for ourselves and for others. Good leaders make decisions and act on them. When they find that they have made a bad decision, they choose another course. Great leaders—or anyone else, for that matter—are rarely judged on one decision. We value people on their overall performance. Failure is only a continuing source of stress when we don't learn from our mistakes. Deciding and acting diminishes the negative energy of stress. Ambivalence and indecision only increase it. He who hesitates is not only lost, he is stressed.

## 39. Be a Little Worldly.

We are all human. What someone else has experienced can also happen to us. Life is not fair. Bonding with others reduces stress by encouraging social support. Social support buffers the impact of inevitable stress. So, don't be afraid to expand your horizons and your social set to help you develop new ways to cope with stress.

## 40. Ventilate.

Accumulated stress eats away at us like an abscess at a bone. We must express how we feel, even if nothing can be done about it. Whom we ventilate with depends on what we wish to talk about. We must speak with the appropriate person, such as a spouse, sibling, or trusted friend, and not hesitate to seek expert advice from a mental health professional, social worker, or pastoral counselor if we need it.

Remember, we can't keep everything inside. One study found that those who did not openly grieve after they lost someone in a tragic fire in Boston in the early 1940s developed psychological symptoms months or years later.

## 41. Improve Interpersonal Skill.

Assertiveness training is one of many ways of making relationships works for us. Assertiveness training can teach us techniques for increasing our own self-esteem. These techniques include learning how to confront others to get what you want without being overbearing or insulting. But they also teach you how to have satisfactory relationships with your more aggressive peers or loved ones without sacrificing your own self-image. Seeking out relationships that help rather than hinder success is critical to stress reduction. We don't need someone saying, "I told you so." We want people in our lives who support risk-taking, creative thinking, and our success. Active listening and time management are other priorities in improving our interpersonal skills.

## 42. Treat People Like Human Beings.

Make yourself available to help others through their times of stress. They need you to listen and to help. This works both ways: When *you* are experiencing stress, your friends (if they are true friends) will be available to help you. Also, helping others deal with their stress will give you the confidence and ability to cope better with your own.

## 43. Dress Up, Not Down.

People like to look at well-dressed people. As Comedian Billy Crystal says, "You look good, you feel good." It facilitates communication. It is a sign of respect for yourself and for the people around you. Clothes not only proclaimeth the man and woman, they can reduce stress by silently affirming your importance and self-worth.

## 44. Be Flexible.

There are a number of ways to master a task. Your own way may not be the best way, or your way (albeit best) may not be feasible. If you feel that everything has to be your way, then you will be miserable when everything doesn't go according to your plan. Your only goal should be getting the job done. Being flexible also involves modifying your schedule or your goals—no one can predict the outside influences that can, and often do, change our plans.

## 45. Don't Gossip.

Gossiping creates enemies and distrust. It's also a good way to lose friends. If you gossip with someone, they may wonder if you gossip about them. There are enough problems in life without having to counter a reputation as a gossip. Friends reduce stress. Enemies enhance it. You don't need to bolster the number who are unhappy with you by gossiping about them.

# V. Workplace Skills

Most of us spend as much time at work as we do at home or with our families. And, when we're not at work, the problems we may be having there can occupy the time we should be using for relaxation and recharging. Here are a few ways to help reduce the workload of workplace stressors.

## 46. Delegate Work.

Successful people are usually successful because they have assumed responsibility for getting things done. However, when they advance to a higher level, it is impossible to do everything themselves. This can often mean something won't get done until they identify people who do the job well. This can be a double-edged sword for some "new managers," since such people are usually good and reliable workers who would like to advance themselves someday.

It is ironic that what can successfully reduce stress at one time in a career (i.e., doing everything yourself) may be the wrong response at another time (i.e., when you *have* to delegate work to get it done). Don't let the need to delegate work be a source of stress. If you successfully delegate, and the work is done properly, you will be recognized because you have developed a whole new set of skills—managing people well—that enables you to advance even further.

## 47. Make Your Weaknesses Strengths.

Don't apologize for your life experiences. Flaunt them as your strengths. A prominent psychoanalyst once told a psychiatric resident selection committee that the best candidates are slightly depressed, since depressed people listen better. If you have been criticized for working too hard, realize that there are many people who feel America is losing its prominence because Americans don't work hard enough.

Sometimes our pain (e.g., depression) or our adaptation to pain (e.g., workaholism) can help us reduce stress by making us stronger. Through crosses and losses we become humbler and wiser.

## 48. Create Buffer Zones Around Anticipated Stresses.

If you're walking into a stressful situation, like asking your hard-nosed boss for a raise, try role-playing with a friend first. Try a few different scenarios. What if your boss says no? What if your boss just laughs at you? What do you say? After this role-playing exercise, try to take your mind off your boss: Go for a walk, go to lunch, read the newspaper. Later, meet with your role-playing friend to review the exercise. Role-playing exercises help you to prepare for stressful situations. And when you're prepared, you'll be more relaxed. Now, go ahead and meet with your boss, but only after you've scheduled time to relax (and role-play) beforehand.

## 49. Prepare.

Remember the Boy Scout motto: Be Prepared. If it's going to rain, wear a raincoat and bring an umbrella. You don't need the unexpected stress of presenting yourself for a job interview soaked to the skin, disheveled, angry, and stressed. Anticipate problems and prepare. Often, while we focus on the big events (like the job interview), it is the little things (like not having an umbrella) that cause big stress.

## 50. Communicate to Those Around You So You Can Get Things Done.

Reduce stress and increase productivity the same way a good football coach does with his team: To achieve victory, all the players must know their role and when and how to play it. Less confusion means less tension on the job. If you're a supervisor, make sure you assign intelligible tasks with clearcut deadlines. This is especially important in large hospitals, law offices, and families, where many jobs must be done efficiently so that people are free to handle the unexpected. In a hospital this might mean freeing a doctor to handle an emergency; in a family, it could mean freeing the parents to spend some unplanned, spontaneous time with their children. Remember, lack of clarity leads to lost time and increased stress.

## 51. Structure Your Environment to Work for You.

If being caught in traffic leaves you frazzled, park your car and take a train or bus. Better yet, live near the bus station or railroad station so you can walk or take a cab. Best of all, live near your work. This may not be possible in many places. But you can still save yourself stress by living near shopping areas, schools, or friends, thereby reducing your travel time. Make life easier by making your environment function for you. If shopping is stressful, buy more than you need so you won't have to shop as much. Don't buy four rolls of toilet paper; buy 12 and save two trips. Do you find shopping for clothes a hassle? Buy ten white shirts rather than one. Or buy your clothes through mail-order houses. If you have more clothes, like shirts and underwear, you save time going to the cleaner and doing the laundry.

## 52. Use Modern Technology.

Secretaries have historically run interference for busy executives by screening phone calls and appointments. Why not do the same at home with an answering machine? You can listen in and decide whether or not you want to pick up the phone. If you are busy, let it wait. When you're not at home, you can call your answering machine or service, see who called, and decide who to call back.

# VI. Learn to Relax and Contemplate

The simplest ways to reduce stress can be summed up easily: Stop, sit down, take a moment, take a deep breath and relax. As the old saying goes, sit back and smell the roses. Here are some final ways to use relaxation and contemplation to make stress work for you.

## 53. Practice Progressive Muscle Relaxation.

A number of relaxation techniques have been developed to reduce stress. These techniques help us "wind down" and can be employed throughout the workday.

One method involves finding a quiet place to sit, closing your eyes, systematically relaxing your muscles from toes to face, and breathing in and out slowly for ten to twenty minutes. Afterward, you sit quietly. This is practiced once or twice a day, but not within two hours of a meal, because digestion appears to interrupt the process. This process allows us to become aware of the sensation of stress in muscles and the feeling of relaxation. Eventually we learn to relax at will.

Differential relaxation (relaxing selected muscles), conditioned relaxation (relaxing to a cue word), and passive relaxation (relaxation without first creating tension) are variations of this technique. In all these, a quiet environment and a passive attitude are essential. You should not scrutinize or grade your own performance.

## 54. Meditate.

Meditation involves focusing concentration and reducing external input. Learning how to focus attention in meditation has a number of benefits.

Studies show that transcendental meditation helps work adjustment by reducing tension, and can lead to increased productivity by improving attention and increasing mental capacity, reaction time, and alertness. Physiological changes with meditation are the opposite of those of the fight-or-flight response described in chapter five.

Transcendental meditation (TM), the best-known method, involves repetition of a secret mantra or prayer word. The word should be one syllable. A decrease in metabolic rate, blood pressure, heart rate, and oxygen use is reported with this technique. Scientific studies have also shown remarkable decrease in incidence of heart attack in people who practice TM regularly.

## 55. Practice Self-Hypnosis, Yoga, or Zen.

Yoga, Zen and self-hypnosis are excellent ways to reduce stress. The goal of yoga is to prepare the body, through selected postures, for spiritual perfection by deleting the superfluous and the mundane. Breathing deeply, slowly, and silently is key. Zen is a religion in which meditation is practiced and which teaches that good moral behavior will lead to a state of enlightenment or nirvana. Self-hypnosis is the desire to achieve the hypnotic state to improve one's life.

All of these techniques help us relax. As we unwind, we can imagine that we come and go like the sea, or float freely like a cloud. This brief mental vacation can help you turn your positive thoughts into positive actions.

Yoga is especially useful for reducing stress because it concentrates on the removal of outside pressures. Even if you don't practice yoga, you can benefit from its main technique: Breathing deeply, slowly, and silently. Many people who have no knowledge of yoga use deep breathing as a valuable tool to help them relax.

## 56. Get Massaged.

Our bodies and psyches under stress are analogous to a taut rubber band; the more we stretch it, the sooner it will break. Massage, like rest, reduces tension in our muscles, even those involuntary muscles that are in our hearts, stomachs, and blood vessels. The less tension we begin with, the greater the tension we can handle.

Massage makes us more aware of our body and how our body changes. William James defined emotion as our awareness of bodily change. We see a bear, we run for our lives, and then the emotion of terror sets in. We do not see the bear, stop to consider how afraid we are, and then run. In the first instance, while we are running we certainly are afraid, but we *use* our fear to help us run faster. Massage relaxes our bodies and puts us in touch with our emotions. It helps us to respond faster and more effectively to the many challenges we encounter.

## 57. Seek Spiritual Nourishment.

We all need spirituality in our lives. Even if you don't believe in a god, you still need to find something that transcends the pain of the moment. You can believe in a power that is greater than your own, like the power of friendship or love. If you believe in the Judeo-Christian God, then "In His will is our peace," as Dante counseled us in *The Divine Comedy*. Whatever your belief, when you're under stress, the concept of a higher power is a big help.

Being a member of a spiritual community has more practical benefits as well: close friendships based on shared values; relaxed activities in a non-competitive atmosphere; the availability of trusted counsel; and simply the reassurance of belonging to a group in a world that too often makes us feel vulnerable and alone.

## 58. Build in Relaxation Time.

We all need "time out." This relaxation time should be built into your schedule. For some, it may be walking one hour to and from work. For others, it may be taking a train rather than driving, and finding new time to study a language or read a book or take a bubble bath or massage. Some executives have a "play day" once a month with a friend to unwind. Building in time "to smell the roses" reduces the regrets of passing years. One retired surgeon wistfully stated, "I never knew my children, and now that I have the time, they don't want me to know my grandchildren."

## 59. Slow Down.

It's easier said than done. People don't usually succeed at this unless they make a real effort to do so. Slowing down may require getting away, blocking off hours on your calendar to catch up, answer telephone calls, or get to know your children. You must decide what pace is right for you. Heart attacks, high blood pressure, or car accidents force us to slow down. Slow down yourself before your body does it for you.

## 60. Abdicate Control at Times in Your Life.

While many of the techniques and simple ways to make stress work for you tell you how to avoid problems, that's not always the answer or the right path. Sometimes you just have to say, "What the heck—let's go for it!" In many ways this is the ultimate way to make stress work for you because it's your choice to plunge in unreservedly. Remember, letting go is enjoyable. Self-abandonment is the secret to the joy of dance, of art, of sexual orgasm, and of religious ecstasy. For brief moments, we become at one with someone or something greater than ourselves. We lose control. It is exciting. It is spiritual. And it is relaxing. Afterward, we are again in control, and better able to function.

# 8

## *A Last Word*

One final thought: Making stress work for you won't be achieved only by following a recipe of sixty ways, or seventy ways, or even one thousand ways. Turning the natural stresses of life to your advantage involves combining awareness of physical health, nutrition, exercise, your home or workplace environment, and interpersonal relationships into a personal plan of your own for stress reduction. After a while, you'll develop your own style, techniques, and "tricks" that will become a part of a new and rewarding lifestyle. As you learn to make stress work for you, you'll see many new advantages to old situations you once thought were to be avoided at all costs. You'll be a healthier and happier person as soon as you learn to make stress work for you!

For more information and sources of help for coping with stress, call Dr. Slaby at 908–522–7045.

# Sources

1. Benson, H: Your innate asset for combating stress. *Harvard Business Review*, 52:49–60, 1974.

2. Cooper, GL; Crump, J: Prevention and coping with occupational stress. *J Occup Med*, 20:420–426, 1978.

3. Dunnett, W; Williams, J: Strength through stress: stress can be turned around to work for you. *Runners World*, pp. 55–57 1980.

4. Fischer, C: Ways to beat stress. *Family Safety*, pp. 8–11, 1980.

5. Gentry, S: *Relaxation: A Natural High*. Center City, Minnesota, Hazelden, 1981.

6. Giordano, DA; Everly, GS: *Controlling Stress*

*and Tension: A Holistic Approach.* Englewood Cliffs, N.J., Prentice Hall, 1979.

7. Gold, MS: *The Good News About Depression.* New York, Bantam Books, 1988.

8. McGaffey, TN: New horizons in organizational stress prevention approaches. *Personal Administrator,* pp. 25–32, November, 1978.

9. Murphy, LR: Worksite stress management programs. *EAP Digest,* pp. 22–25, 1982.

10. Pesci, M: Stress management: separating myth from reality. *Personnel Administrator,* pp. 57–67, 1982.

11. Peters, RK; Benson, H: Time out from tension. *Harvard Business Review,* 56: 120–124, 1978.

12. Raskies, E; Avard, J: Teaching healthy managers to control their economy-prone (type A) behavior, in *Self Modification of Emotional Behavior* (edited by Blakenstein, K; Polivus, J). New York, Plenum Press, 1982.

13. Slaby, AE: Crisis-oriented therapy. *New Directions in Emergency Psychiatry,* 28:21–34, 1985.

14. Slaby, AE; Lieb, J; Tancredi, LR: *The Handbook of Psychiatric Emergencies*. New York, Elsevier, 1985.

## ABOUT THE AUTHOR

ANDREW E. SLABY, M.D., Ph.D., M.P.H.

Dr. Andrew Slaby is a nationally prominent epidemiologist, psychiatrist, and specialist in human behavior. Medical Director of Fair Oaks Hospital, Summit, N.J., Dr. Slaby is also Adjunct Professor of Psychiatry and Human Behavior at Brown University and Clinical Professor of Psychiatry at New York University and The New York Medical College. Dr. Slaby is the author of numerous scientific books, papers, and research studies. Frequently appearing as an expert on television and radio programs, Dr. Slaby lectures on personal crisis intervention/management, depression, suicide prevention, management of violent individuals, and techniques people can use to adapt to life-threatening stress or illness. He also writes and lectures on the management of stress in adolescents and college-age individuals. The recipient of many scientific prizes and awards, Dr. Slaby is a graduate of Columbia University's College of Physicians and Surgeons and of Yale University.

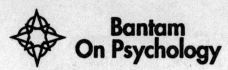

# Bantam
# On Psychology

☐ 28037-6 **MEN WHO HATE WOMEN &
THE WOMEN WHO LOVE THEM**
Dr. Susan Forward                                              $5.99

☐ 26401-X **MORE HOPE AND HELP FOR YOUR NERVES**
Claire Weekes                                                   $4.50

☐ 27043-5 **THE POWER OF THE SUBCONSCIOUS MIND**
Dr. J. Murphy                                                   $4.50

☐ 34367-X **TEACH ONLY LOVE** Gerald Jampolsky, M.D.
(A Large Format Book)                                           $8.95

## ALSO AVAILABLE ON AUDIO CASSETTE

☐ 45142-1 **WHEN AM I GOING TO BE HAPPY? BREAK THE
EMOTIONAL BAD HABITS THAT KEEP YOU FROM
REACHING YOUR POTENTIAL**
Penelope Russianoff, Ph.D                                       $8.95

☐ 45167-7 **TEACH ONLY LOVE** Gerald Jampolsky                  $8.95

☐ 45218-5 **LIFE IS UNCERTAIN, EAT DESSERT FIRST: Finding
the Joy You Deserve**
Sol Gordon and Harold Brecher                                   $8.95